Introduction

A. The Allure of Travel

Have you ever felt the irresistible allure of travel? The thrill of discovering new places, savoring exotic cuisines, and immersing yourself in diverse cultures? Traveling opens a world of possibilities, igniting our wanderlust, and reminding us of the beauty and wonder that this planet holds. It's a journey of self-discovery, a celebration of human connection, and an exploration of the unknown.

B. The Myth of Expensive Travel

Yet, for many, this allure is dampened by the myth of expensive travel. You've probably heard it before: "Traveling is only for the wealthy," or "You need to empty your savings to see the world." It's a misconception that has deterred countless dreamers from pursuing their travel aspirations. But here's the truth: Traveling on a budget is not only possible; it can be immensely rewarding and life-changing.

C. Purpose of the Ebook

This ebook, "Traveling on a Budget: Explore the World Affordably," is your roadmap to shattering the myth of expensive travel. Our purpose here is clear—to empower you with the knowledge, strategies, and inspiration needed to embark on budget-friendly adventures. We want to show you that exploring the world doesn't have to drain your bank account; it can actually enrich your life in more ways than you can imagine.

So, whether you're a seasoned traveler looking to trim your expenses or someone who's never ventured beyond their comfort zone due to budget concerns, this ebook is your gateway to fulfilling your travel dreams without breaking the bank. Join us on this journey as we unravel the secrets of affordable travel and embark on a path to explore the world, one budget-friendly adventure at a time.

Let's begin our adventure together!

Chapter 1: Planning Your Budget Adventure

"The journey of a thousand miles begins with a single step." - Lao Tzu

A. Setting Your Travel Goals

Before you pack your bags and set off on your budget adventure, it's crucial to define your travel goals. What do you hope to achieve with your journey? What experiences do you seek? Setting clear goals will not only give purpose to your travels but also help you tailor your budget accordingly.

1. Identify Your Objectives: Are you seeking relaxation on a beach, cultural immersion,

adventure, or perhaps a mix of everything? Understanding your primary objectives will guide your destination choices and activities.

2. Budget Priorities: Determine your priorities within your budget. Would you rather splurge on unique experiences, like a hot air balloon ride, or prioritize saving on accommodations and meals? Knowing where you're willing to spend more or cut back is essential.

B. Creating a Travel Budget

Your travel budget is the foundation of your budget adventure. By carefully planning your finances, you can ensure that you have the means to explore without worry. Here's how to create an effective travel budget:

1. Calculate Total Expenses: Estimate all your travel expenses, including transportation, accommodation, food, activities, and incidentals

like travel insurance and visas. Consider currency exchange rates if you're going abroad.

2. Set a Realistic Budget: Determine how much you're willing to spend overall. Be realistic and ensure it aligns with your financial capabilities. A well-structured budget will keep you on track.

3. Track Your Spending: Use budgeting apps or spreadsheets to track your expenses during your journey. This will help you stay within your budget and make necessary adjustments if needed.

4. Emergency Fund: Allocate a portion of your budget to an emergency fund. Unexpected expenses can arise, and having a financial safety net will reduce stress.

C. Choosing Budget-Friendly Destinations

Selecting the right destination plays a pivotal role in ensuring an affordable adventure. Here's how to identify budget-friendly destinations:

1. Research Costs: Use travel websites and forums to research the cost of living, accommodation, and activities in potential destinations. Some regions are naturally more budget-friendly than others.

2. Consider Off-Peak Seasons: Traveling during off-peak seasons can lead to significant savings on accommodations and flights. Plus, you'll avoid crowds, making for a more enjoyable experience.

3. Local Currency Strength: Pay attention to currency exchange rates. A favorable exchange rate can stretch your budget further in some countries.

4. Hidden Gems: Look beyond the tourist hotspots. Smaller towns and cities often offer more affordable options and a chance to immerse yourself in local culture.

Remember, budget travel is not about sacrificing experiences but rather about making conscious choices that align with your goals and financial situation. In the following chapters, we'll delve deeper into specific strategies for finding affordable accommodations, transportation, and dining options, allowing you to embark on your budget adventure with confidence and excitement.

Chapter 2: Finding Affordable Accommodation

"A journey of a thousand miles begins with a comfy place to rest."

A. Options for Budget Lodging

Affordable accommodation doesn't mean compromising on comfort or safety. There are various options tailored to budget travelers:

1. Hostels: Hostels are a classic choice for budget-conscious travelers. They offer dormitory-style rooms and communal spaces where you can meet fellow adventurers. Some hostels also provide private rooms at a fraction of the cost of hotels.

2. Guesthouses: Guesthouses or guest lodges are often family-run and provide cozy, budget-friendly rooms. They offer a more personal and local experience compared to larger hotels.

3. Motels: In many countries, motels are a cost-effective alternative to hotels. They're often situated along highways and cater to travelers on road trips.

4. Budget Hotels: Look for budget hotel chains or independently-owned budget hotels. These establishments offer clean and comfortable rooms without the high price tag.

5. Camping: If you enjoy the great outdoors, consider camping. Campgrounds are usually more affordable than traditional lodging, and you'll get to experience nature up close.

B. Using Online Booking Platforms

Online booking platforms have revolutionized the way we find and book accommodations. Here's how to make the most of them:

1. Comparison Sites: Utilize hotel comparison websites and apps to compare prices, read reviews, and find the best deals. Some popular options include Booking.com, Expedia, and TripAdvisor.

2. Last-Minute Deals: Keep an eye out for last-minute discounts and deals. Many booking platforms offer special rates for spontaneous travelers.

3. Membership Discounts: Consider joining loyalty programs or membership platforms that offer discounts and exclusive deals for accommodations. These can lead to significant savings over time.

4. Flexible Booking: Opt for flexible booking options that allow you to change or cancel

reservations without hefty fees. This flexibility can be a lifesaver if your plans change.

5. Local Booking Apps: In some regions, local booking apps and websites may offer better deals than international platforms. Don't hesitate to explore these options for hidden gems.

C. Alternative Accommodations (Hostels, Airbnb, Camping)

1. Hostels: Hostels are not just for backpackers. They offer a social atmosphere and often provide communal kitchens, which can help you save on dining expenses. Look for hostels with private rooms if you prefer more privacy.

2. Airbnb: Airbnb allows you to rent private rooms, apartments, or even entire homes. It's often more affordable than hotels and offers a local perspective on your destination.

3. Camping: Camping is a budget-friendly way to connect with nature. Research campgrounds in advance, and make sure you have the necessary gear. Some national parks offer low-cost camping facilities.

4. House Sitting: Consider house sitting as a way to stay in a home for free in exchange for taking care of someone's property or pets. Websites like TrustedHousesitters can help you find opportunities.

5. Couchsurfing: Couchsurfing connects travelers with locals who offer free accommodations on their couches or spare rooms. It's a fantastic way to meet new people and save on lodging costs.

Finding affordable accommodation is a crucial step in your budget adventure. By exploring these options and using online tools wisely, you'll discover that comfortable and budget-friendly places to stay are abundant, allowing you to fully enjoy your travels without financial stress. In the next chapter, we'll delve into tips for securing budget-friendly transportation options.

Chapter 3: Navigating Transportation on a Budget

"The journey not the arrival matters." - T.S. Eliot

A. Affordable Flight and Train Options

Getting to your destination can often be a significant portion of your travel expenses. Here's how to find budget-friendly options for both flights and trains:

1. Flight Booking Tips:
   - Flexible Dates: Be flexible with your travel dates to take advantage of lower fares on different days of the week.

- Comparison Websites: Use flight comparison websites like Skyscanner, Kayak, or Google Flights to compare prices from various airlines.

- Budget Airlines: Consider flying with budget airlines, which often offer lower fares but may have stricter baggage policies.

- Redeem Miles: If you have frequent flyer miles or credit card rewards, check if you can use them to reduce the cost of your flights.

- Hidden Cities: Explore the concept of "hidden city" ticketing, where booking a flight with a layover in your intended destination is cheaper than a direct flight.

2. Train Travel:

- Rail Passes: In regions like Europe and Japan, rail passes can provide significant savings for multiple train journeys within a set period.

- Advance Booking: Train tickets are often cheaper when booked in advance. Check the train company's official website for deals and discounts.

- Regional Trains: Consider regional or slower trains, which can be more affordable than high-speed options.

B. Utilizing Public Transportation

Once you've reached your destination, public transportation can be a cost-effective and efficient way to get around:

1. City Cards and Passes: Many cities offer tourist cards or transportation passes that provide unlimited travel on buses, trams, and subways for a fixed fee. These can save you money if you plan to use public transport frequently.

2. Local Insights: Ask locals or hotel staff about the best and most economical ways to navigate public transportation. They might have insider tips on cheaper ticket options.

3. Walking and Biking: In smaller cities or towns, walking or renting a bicycle can be an eco-friendly and budget-friendly way to explore.

C. Exploring Ridesharing and Car Rentals

1. Ridesharing Services: Apps like Uber and Lyft offer convenient transportation options in many cities. They can sometimes be more affordable than traditional taxis, especially for short trips.

2. Car Rentals:
   - Comparison Shopping: Compare prices from different car rental companies online. Booking in advance often leads to better deals.
   - Fuel Efficiency: Choose a fuel-efficient vehicle to save on gas costs during your road trips.
   - Insurance Considerations: Be aware of insurance options, and check if your credit card provides rental car insurance to avoid unnecessary costs.

3. Carsharing: Some cities have carsharing programs that allow you to rent a car by the hour or day. This can be a cost-effective option for occasional use.

Navigating transportation on a budget requires a combination of research and flexibility. By exploring various options, booking in advance, and using local transportation wisely, you can keep your travel costs down, leaving you with more resources to enjoy the experiences and adventures that await you at your destination. In the next chapter, we'll dive into strategies for dining affordably while on the road.

Chapter 4: Dining Without Breaking the Bank

"To eat is a necessity, but to eat intelligently is an art." - François de La Rochefoucauld

A. Local Food Markets and Street Food

Exploring the local food scene is not only a culinary adventure but also a budget-friendly way to savor the flavors of your destination:

1. Street Food Stalls: Seek out street food stalls and carts where locals dine. Not only are these often the most authentic culinary experiences, but they're also incredibly budget-friendly.

2. Local Markets: Visit local markets where vendors sell fresh produce, snacks, and ready-to-eat meals. You can pick up fruits, bread, cheese, and other essentials for a picnic or quick, inexpensive meals.

3. Food Tours: Consider joining a food tour led by a local guide. These tours often take you to hidden culinary gems and offer insights into the culture through food.

4. Ask Locals for Recommendations: Don't hesitate to ask locals for their favorite places to eat. They'll likely point you to affordable, beloved eateries.

B. Cooking and Self-Catering

One of the most effective ways to save on dining expenses is to cook your meals:

1. Accommodation with Kitchen Facilities: If you're staying in hostels, guesthouses, or Airbnb

properties, choose ones with kitchen facilities. This allows you to prepare your own meals, saving money on dining out.

2. Local Ingredients: Shop at local grocery stores and markets for fresh ingredients. Experiment with local recipes and flavors to enhance your culinary adventure.

3. Picnics: Enjoy picnics in parks, by the beach, or in scenic spots. It's not only cost-effective but also a lovely way to soak in the surroundings.

4. Meal Planning: Plan your meals and snacks in advance. This prevents impulse spending on food when you're hungry and in a hurry.

C. Finding Budget-Friendly Restaurants

Eating out can still be budget-friendly if you know where to look:

1. Menu du Jour: In many countries, restaurants offer a "menu of the day" with a fixed price for a multi-course meal. It's often a great value.

2. Lunch Specials: Opt for lunch specials or early bird dinners. These are usually more affordable than evening dining.

3. Local Eateries: Dine at local, family-run restaurants away from tourist hotspots. These establishments often offer better value and more authentic dishes.

4. Online Reviews: Use review websites and apps like Yelp, TripAdvisor, or Google Maps to find well-rated budget-friendly restaurants in your area.

5. Happy Hour: Take advantage of happy hour deals, which often include discounted drinks and snacks.

6. Share Meals: If portions are generous, consider sharing dishes with your travel companions. This not only reduces costs but also allows you to taste more variety.

Dining on a budget doesn't mean sacrificing flavor or experience. In fact, it can be an opportunity to savor local delicacies and immerse yourself in the culture of your destination. By exploring street food, cooking your own meals when possible, and choosing wisely when dining out, you can enjoy delicious, budget-friendly cuisine on your travels. In the next chapter, we'll discuss strategies for saving on activities and entertainment while exploring the world on a budget.

Chapter 5: Saving on Activities and Entertainment

"Travel makes one modest. You see what a tiny place you occupy in the world." - Gustave Flaubert

A. Free and Low-Cost Attractions

Exploring a destination doesn't have to break the bank. Many cities and regions offer an array of free or budget-friendly attractions:

1. Museums and Galleries: Look for museums and galleries with free admission days or discounted entry for students, seniors, or youth. Some institutions are always free.

2. Historic Sites: Explore historic sites, monuments, and landmarks, many of which are open to the public at no cost.

3. Parks and Natural Beauty: Spend time in parks, gardens, and natural reserves. Enjoying nature is not only budget-friendly but also rejuvenating.

4. Walking Tours: Join free walking tours provided by local guides or use self-guided tour apps to explore the city on foot. It's an informative and cost-effective way to learn about your surroundings.

5. Local Events: Check local event listings for free concerts, festivals, and cultural events happening during your visit.

B. Discounts and City Passes

Maximize your savings by taking advantage of discounts and city passes:

1. City Passes: Many cities offer tourist passes that provide access to multiple attractions for a fixed fee. They can be excellent value if you plan to visit several sites.

2. Student and Youth Discounts: If you're a student or a young traveler, inquire about discounts at attractions, transportation, and entertainment venues.

3. Senior Discounts: Seniors often receive reduced admission prices at various attractions.

4. Group Discounts: Traveling with friends or family? Look for group discounts, which can significantly reduce expenses.

5. Online Deals: Purchase tickets in advance online to benefit from discounts and skip long lines at popular attractions.

C. Engaging in Budget-Friendly Experiences

Immerse yourself in local culture without overspending:

1. Attend Local Workshops: Participate in workshops or classes that teach you about the local culture, such as cooking, dance, or traditional crafts. These experiences often provide valuable insights and memorable moments.

2. Volunteer Opportunities: Look for volunteer opportunities or cultural exchange programs that allow you to contribute to the community while learning about their way of life.

3. Local Markets and Street Performers: Spend time at local markets, where you can enjoy street performances, sample local food, and interact with vendors and artisans.

4. Off-the-Beaten-Path Exploration: Explore less-visited neighborhoods and areas. You'll often find unique, budget-friendly experiences away from tourist crowds.

5. Public Events: Check out public events, such as parades, fairs, or religious ceremonies. These can provide an authentic cultural experience.

By seeking out free and low-cost attractions, leveraging discounts and city passes, and engaging in immersive, budget-friendly experiences, you'll be able to enjoy your destination to the fullest without straining your budget. In the next chapter, we'll explore additional money-saving tips and hacks to enhance your budget travel journey.

Chapter 6: Money-Saving Tips and Hacks

"Adventure may hurt you but monotony will kill you." - Unknown

A. Traveling During Off-Peak Seasons

Timing can significantly impact the cost of your journey. Here's why traveling during off-peak seasons can be a budget-savvy choice:

1. Lower Prices: Accommodations, flights, and attractions often offer reduced rates during less popular travel times. You can score significant savings.

2. Fewer Crowds: Avoiding peak seasons means fewer tourists and shorter lines at popular attractions, enhancing your overall experience.

3. Local Immersion: Off-peak travel allows you to interact more with locals, giving you a more authentic understanding of the destination.

4. Flexibility: Traveling during less busy times can offer more flexibility in your itinerary. You can be spontaneous and make changes as you go.

B. Using Travel Rewards and Loyalty Programs

Maximize your budget by tapping into travel rewards and loyalty programs:

1. Credit Card Rewards: Use travel rewards credit cards to earn points or miles on everyday expenses. These can be redeemed for flights, hotel stays, and more.

2. Hotel Loyalty Programs: Join hotel loyalty programs to earn free nights and enjoy exclusive perks like room upgrades or complimentary breakfasts.

3. Frequent Flyer Programs: Sign up for frequent flyer programs with airlines you frequently use. Accumulate miles for future flights and enjoy member benefits.

4. Travel Insurance Benefits: Some travel insurance policies offer coverage for trip cancellations or interruptions, potentially saving you money if your plans change unexpectedly.

5. Cashback Programs: Explore cashback programs that refund a portion of your travel expenses when you book through their platforms.

C. Currency Exchange and Banking Tips

Efficiently managing your money while abroad is essential for budget travelers:

1. Avoid Airport Currency Exchange: Airport kiosks often offer unfavorable exchange rates. Exchange currency at local banks or ATMs for better rates.

2. ATM Withdrawals: Use ATMs to withdraw local currency as needed. Check with your bank for partners abroad to avoid ATM fees.

3. No Foreign Transaction Fee Cards: Carry credit or debit cards that do not charge foreign transaction fees to save on currency conversion costs.

4. Notify Your Bank: Inform your bank of your travel plans to prevent them from flagging your transactions as suspicious when abroad.

5. Carry Local Currency: Keep a small amount of local currency for immediate expenses upon arrival, such as transportation or food.

6. Currency Converter Apps: Download currency converter apps to quickly calculate exchange rates and make informed spending decisions.

By applying these money-saving tips and hacks, you can make your budget stretch further, allowing you to indulge in more experiences and make the most of your travel adventures. In the next chapter, we'll discuss essential tips for staying safe and healthy while exploring the world on a budget.

Chapter 7: Staying Safe and Healthy

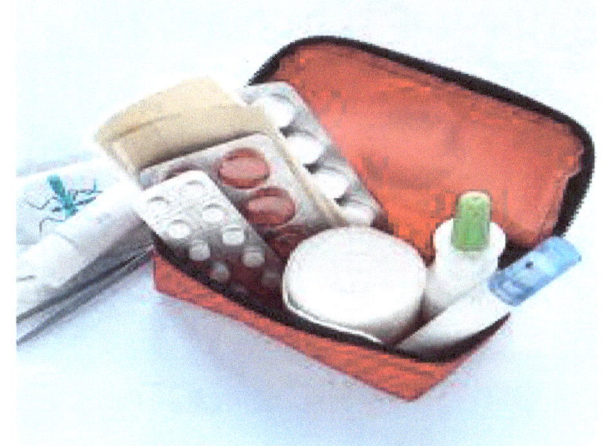

"Health is the greatest possession. Contentment is the greatest treasure. Confidence is the greatest friend." - Lao Tzu

A. Travel Insurance Considerations

1. Importance of Travel Insurance: Travel insurance is not an optional expense; it's a vital investment in your well-being. It provides financial protection against unexpected events, such as trip cancellations, medical emergencies, or lost luggage.

2. Types of Travel Insurance: Explore various types of travel insurance, including trip

cancellation/interruption insurance, medical coverage, and comprehensive plans. Choose the one that aligns with your travel needs and budget.

3. Read the Fine Print: Carefully read the policy details to understand what's covered, policy limits, and any exclusions. Ensure it covers activities you plan to engage in during your trip.

4. Emergency Assistance: Verify if the policy includes 24/7 emergency assistance. This service can be invaluable in case you need medical help or face travel disruptions.

B. Health Precautions and Vaccinations

1. Consult a Healthcare Professional: Before your trip, schedule a visit to your healthcare provider or a travel clinic. Discuss necessary vaccinations and health precautions based on your destination.

2. Routine Vaccinations: Ensure your routine vaccinations, such as measles, mumps, rubella, and influenza, are up to date.

3. Travel-Specific Vaccinations: Depending on your destination, you may need vaccinations for diseases like hepatitis, typhoid, or yellow fever. Some countries require proof of vaccination for entry.

4. Prescription Medications: If you take prescription medications, bring an ample supply for your trip and keep them in their original containers with clear labels. Check if your medications are allowed in your destination country.

5. Travel Health Kit: Pack a basic travel health kit with essentials like pain relievers, antidiarrheal medication, adhesive bandages, and any prescription medications.

C. Personal Safety Tips

1. Research Local Laws: Familiarize yourself with the laws and customs of your destination. Respect local regulations and cultural norms.

2. Stay Informed: Keep an eye on travel advisories and local news. Stay informed about any potential safety concerns in your destination.

3. Stay Connected: Share your travel itinerary with friends or family and maintain communication with someone back home. Provide them with your contact information and emergency contacts.

4. Secure Your Belongings: Protect your belongings by using anti-theft bags, locks, and safes in your accommodation. Be cautious when using public Wi-Fi for online transactions.

5. Avoid Risky Areas: Stay away from areas with a history of crime or civil unrest. Use reliable transportation options, and avoid walking alone at night in unfamiliar places.

6. Travel Insurance for Personal Safety: Ensure your travel insurance includes coverage for emergency medical evacuation and repatriation in case of serious illness or injury.

Staying safe and healthy is paramount when traveling, regardless of your budget. By carefully considering travel insurance, taking necessary health precautions, and following personal safety tips, you can explore the world with confidence and peace of mind. In the next chapter, we'll explore tips for packing smart and efficiently for your budget travel adventure.

Chapter 8: Packing Smart for Budget Travel

"Pack light, travel far, and live long."

A. Minimalist Packing Strategies

1. Less is More: Embrace the philosophy of minimalism when packing. Aim to bring only what you truly need. Remember, you can buy or borrow items locally if necessary.

2. Mix-and-Match Wardrobe: Pack versatile clothing items that can be mixed and matched to create different outfits. Neutral colors and classic styles work well.

3. Laundry Options: Plan for laundry facilities at your destination. You can pack fewer clothes and simply wash them during your trip.

4. Roll, Don't Fold: Rolling your clothes instead of folding them can save space and reduce wrinkles in your garments.

5. Compression Bags: Consider using compression bags or packing cubes to maximize suitcase space and keep your belongings organized.

B. Must-Have Travel Essentials

1. Travel Documents: Keep essential documents organized, including your passport, visa, travel insurance, itinerary, and any required entry forms.

2. Money and Payment Methods: Carry some local currency, a credit/debit card with no foreign transaction fees, and a backup source of funds, like a travel money card.

3. Electronics: Pack necessary electronics such as your smartphone, charger, adapter, and power bank. Don't forget a universal adapter for international travel.

4. Travel-Sized Toiletries: Use travel-sized toiletries to save space and comply with airline regulations. Remember essentials like toothpaste, a toothbrush, shampoo, and soap.

5. First-Aid Kit: Include basic first-aid supplies like bandages, pain relievers, and any prescription medications.

6. Travel Pillow and Eye Mask: These can make long journeys more comfortable and help you rest during flights or train rides.

C. Packing for Different Climates

1. Layering: If you're traveling to a destination with varying temperatures, pack clothing that can be

layered. This allows you to adapt to changing weather conditions.

2. Research Weather: Check the weather forecast for your destination and pack accordingly. Be prepared for rain or unexpected weather changes.

3. Versatile Outerwear: Invest in a versatile, lightweight jacket or coat that can be used in multiple climates. A good-quality jacket can last you throughout your travels.

4. Footwear: Choose comfortable, versatile shoes suitable for various terrains. Consider packing sandals for warm weather and sturdy walking shoes for exploring.

5. Climate-Specific Items: If you're traveling to extreme climates, such as a snowy region or a tropical paradise, make sure you have the appropriate gear and clothing.

Remember that packing smart not only saves space and weight but can also help you avoid baggage fees, reduce stress during travel, and ensure you have everything you need for a comfortable journey. In the next chapter, we'll explore how to embrace cultural immersion while staying on budget during your travels.

Chapter 9: Embracing Cultural Immersion

"Travel makes one modest. You see what a tiny place you occupy in the world." - Gustave Flaubert

A. Interacting with Locals

1. Open and Respectful: Approach locals with an open and respectful attitude. Show genuine interest in their culture, traditions, and way of life.

2. Ask Questions: Don't hesitate to ask questions and engage in conversations. Locals often appreciate travelers who are curious about their world.

3. Local Cuisine: Try local dishes and street food. Dining where the locals eat is a delicious way to immerse yourself in the culture.

4. Participate in Local Activities: Join community events, festivals, or cultural workshops. This allows you to experience the culture firsthand and create lasting memories.

B. Learning the Language Basics

1. Greetings and Common Phrases: Learning a few basic greetings and common phrases in the local language can go a long way. Locals often appreciate your effort to communicate in their language.

2. Language Apps: Use language learning apps and phrasebooks to improve your language skills. Many apps offer offline capabilities, making them handy while traveling.

3. Language Exchange: Consider language exchange meetups with locals or fellow travelers. It's a great way to practice and learn from each other.

4. Local Etiquette: Familiarize yourself with local customs and etiquette to show respect for the culture. For example, learn how to properly greet, tip, or address people.

C. Engaging in Sustainable Tourism

1. Respect the Environment: Dispose of waste responsibly and avoid single-use plastics. Participate in local conservation efforts, such as beach cleanups or wildlife protection programs.

2. Support Local Businesses: Choose locally-owned accommodations, restaurants, and shops to directly contribute to the community's economy.

3. Responsible Wildlife Tourism: If you encounter wildlife, maintain a respectful distance and do not engage in activities that harm or stress animals.

4. Cultural Sensitivity: Respect cultural norms and traditions, even if they differ from your own. Dress modestly when visiting religious sites, and ask for permission before taking photos of individuals.

5. Eco-Friendly Transportation: Opt for eco-friendly transportation options like biking or walking when exploring the area. Use public transport or carpool when possible.

Cultural immersion not only enriches your travel experience but also fosters connections and understanding between you and the locals. By interacting respectfully, learning some local language, and practicing sustainable tourism, you can make a positive impact on the places you visit while enjoying an authentic and budget-friendly adventure. In the final chapter, we'll conclude our journey with tips on budget travel planning and organization.

Chapter 10: Post-Trip Reflection and Next Adventures

"Adventure is worthwhile in itself." - Amelia Earhart

A. Keeping a Travel Journal

1. Capture Memories: Reflect on your journey by keeping a travel journal. Write about your experiences, thoughts, and emotions. Include details like local encounters, memorable meals, and unexpected discoveries.

2. Photos and Mementos: Attach photos, postcards, and mementos to your journal entries.

These visual reminders will transport you back to your travel experiences.

3. Learn and Grow: Use your journal as a tool for personal growth. Write about what you've learned from your adventures and how they've changed you.

4. Future Inspiration: Your travel journal can serve as inspiration for future trips. Reading about past adventures may reignite your passion for budget travel.

B. Budgeting for Future Trips

1. Reflect on Expenses: Review your past travel expenses to gain insights into your spending patterns. Identify areas where you can cut costs or allocate more budget for experiences you value most.

2. Set Financial Goals: Establish specific financial goals for your future trips. Determine how much

you need to save and create a savings plan with deadlines.

3. Travel Fund: Open a dedicated travel fund or savings account. Automatically transfer money into this account each month to steadily grow your travel budget.

4. Cut Unnecessary Expenses: Analyze your daily expenses and eliminate non-essential items. Redirect the money you save toward your travel fund.

C. Encouragement to Continue Budget Travel

1. Reflect on the Benefits: Think about the positive aspects of budget travel. It not only allows you to see the world but also fosters resourcefulness, adaptability, and a deeper appreciation for experiences over possessions.

2. Stay Inspired: Follow travel blogs, read books, and connect with other budget travelers online.

Surround yourself with sources of inspiration and support.

3. Plan Your Next Adventure: Start researching and planning your next budget travel adventure. Having a new destination in mind can motivate you to continue saving and exploring.

4. Join Travel Communities: Join travel forums or social media groups where budget travelers share tips, stories, and encouragement. Connect with like-minded individuals who share your passion for exploration.

5. Celebrate Your Achievements: Recognize and celebrate your achievements as a budget traveler. Whether it's conquering a challenging trek or mastering the art of haggling, acknowledge your growth and accomplishments.

Budget travel isn't just a way to see the world affordably; it's a mindset and a lifestyle that can lead to a lifetime of enriching experiences.

Embrace the lessons learned, continue setting goals, and keep exploring new horizons. Your journey as a budget traveler is a remarkable adventure that will continue to inspire and shape your life.

Additional Resources

A. Recommended Websites and Apps

1. Skyscanner: An excellent platform for comparing flight prices, finding the cheapest options, and setting fare alerts.

2. Google Flights: A user-friendly tool for exploring flight options and tracking airfare trends.

3. Kayak: Offers comprehensive search options for flights, hotels, car rentals, and more.

4. Hostelworld: A go-to website for finding budget-friendly hostels and accommodations worldwide.

5. Airbnb: Allows you to book unique and affordable accommodations, including apartments and homes.

6. Rome2rio: Helps you plan your transportation routes by showing various options and prices between destinations.

7. Couchsurfing: A platform for connecting with locals who offer free accommodation, cultural exchange, and unique experiences.

8. Google Maps: A versatile app for navigation, finding local eateries, and public transportation routes.

9. Duolingo: A language-learning app that offers free lessons in multiple languages, perfect for brushing up on language basics.

10. Trail Wallet: An expense tracking app designed for travelers to monitor their budget on the go.

B. Travel Communities and Forums

1. Lonely Planet's Thorn Tree Forum: A popular travel forum where you can ask questions, share advice, and connect with fellow travelers.

2. TripAdvisor Forums: Offers a wide range of forums covering destinations, travel tips, and trip planning.

3. Reddit Travel Community (r/travel): An active community of travelers sharing experiences, recommendations, and advice.

4. Nomadic Matt's Travel Forum: A supportive community created by travel expert Nomadic Matt, with a focus on budget travel.

5. HoboTraveler.com: A community of long-term travelers sharing insights, tips, and resources.

C. Further Reading and References

1. "Vagabonding: An Uncommon Guide to the Art of Long-Term World Travel" by Rolf Potts: A

must-read for those considering long-term budget travel.

2. "The Art of Travel" by Alain de Botton: Explores the philosophical aspects of travel, encouraging deeper connections with destinations.

3. "How to Travel the World on $50 a Day" by Matt Kepnes: Offers practical advice for traveling affordably, based on the author's extensive travel experiences.

4. "The Backpacker Bible: Your Essential Guide to Round the World Travel" by The Broke Backpacker: A comprehensive resource for budget travelers, covering everything from planning to on-the-road tips.

5. "The Budget-Minded Traveler Podcast" by Jackie Nourse: A podcast featuring interviews, tips, and stories from budget-conscious travelers.

These additional resources are valuable tools for enhancing your budget travel experiences, connecting with like-minded adventurers, and gaining further insights into the world of affordable exploration. Happy travels!